Wine-growing France is now experiencing its golden age, in my opinion we are approaching a real turning point. At a time when Bordeaux bashing is in full swing and that of Burgundy is coming, it seems important to me to show how France remains a benchmark for any wine lover.

Why did these bashing happen? The answer is simple: the mismatch between supply and demand. The breakdown between what wine growers have to offer (image, quality, price, recognition and considerations for their consumers versus demand (taste, trend, purchasing power, Eco-bio responsible...).

The aim of this guide is to show how these terroirs are full of pearls under the radar of the general public or certain critics.

This guide allows you each year to discover the TOP3 of the best wines from each region and to discover which are the wines and winemakers of tomorrow to follow in the years to come.

The main objective being as much as possible to introduce new wines to readers, my selection criteria are limited to 2 factors:

- The quality. Of course, there is something subjective about the perception of quality in wine, but the pleasure and emotion shown during repeated tastings allow me to mitigate partially this subjectivity.

- Fame. Again, subjectivity will you tell me .... absolutely and here I fully assume it since my main objective is to highlight the wines under the radar or still under-estimated. Monitoring the digital sphere but also private advices from winegrowers, merchants, friends ..., I estimate each year whether it is still opportune to discuss this or that winegrower and his wines.

So, what are the future talents of tomorrow? well, let's turn the page .... and I wish you a pleasant reading which I hope will be full of good discoveries...

Who am I ?

Do you think you will know the answer at the end of this chapter? Yes and no. Why this ambiguity?

For several reasons, I chose to post wine critics and ranking anonymously after many thoughts. The main one is independence! For decades, I have been exploring the worlds of wine and have developed, like everyone else, a network, experience and tastes. Publishing publicly would change my life. My professional life and my private life. My relationship with the different actors would also inevitably change and that I cannot afford ...

Publishing anonymously also offers me the possibility of freeing myself from advertisements from sponsors or pressures / influences of all kinds. I think that digitalization will gradually offer new horizons in the rigid world of wine criticism. Here, I therefore wanted to initiate a yearly Top X fine wines, not those that we see everywhere, but those are the future gems. Share accessible wines to all (Price or availability) is the purpose. Above all, I wanted to make a guide to discover new talent and shake up the conventional establishment.

So, who am I: Winemaker, Wine Merchant, Famous Wine Critic, Inspector for a famous Restaurant guide? French, English, Swiss, German, Italian...? Regardless, keep in mind that wine is fun to be shared, and this guide is an invitation ...

So, Ladies and Gentlemen, your hidden critic presents now…. The 2021 Guide to Top French fine wines under the radar.

The Masked Wine Critic.

Contents table

Best 2021 Winemaker

Thomas Batardière

Thomas Batardière studied various discipline before starting career in wine. First, he joined a wine merchant oriented to natural wines.

This changed dramatically his life. Direction Beaune to get certificate and he was brought to work in Saumur, at famous Château Yvonne, alongside Mathieu Vallé, where he remained for nearly three years, taking various roles, from the vineyard to the cellar.

In 2011, Thomas set out on his own, buying two hectares of vineyards (Chenin) in Rablay-sur-Layon. Human scale property to maintain high quality level and to remain able to manage all required tasks

Influenced by its conviction and experiences in natural wines, he has converted vines to organic and biodynamic, to obtain, in 2015, Demeter certification. In the cellar, no inputs, no winemaking, just common sense but vinification is here at state of the art. Thomas learned oenology to learn how to do without it.... No troubles with nature vinification, always pure wine without disappointment of some natural wines...

Various grape varieties in those vineyards : Cabernet Franc, Grolleau but wide majority is Chenin, king grape varieties of Loire. Most interesting wines of Thomas are white. And they are not good, they are excellent.

When i discover this winemaker, I feel upset.

Best 2021 Revelation

Olivier Lejeune Clos des Plantes

Olivier manages a low-production but exquisite mineral wines, making him a future icon of the Loire Valley. After 10 years traveling South-East Asia to promote IT solutions dedicated to mobile telephony, Olivier Lejeune has converted to working in the vineyard. One more....

Graduated from a one-year course at the University in New Zealand, he honed his skills in the Felton Road Estate. Like Thomas Batardière, with this baggage, he settled in Anjou, France, where he founded the Clos des Plantes. Olivier Lejeune is a winegrower who skillfully interprets the qualities of the Chenin Blanc grape and produces incredible dry wines with a subtle maturity.

He took over 3 hectares of vines in 2017 (2.5 of Chenin). The vines are located due south, on the place called Montbenault (like the Richard Leroy estate).

As usual, quality starts in the vineyard, Olivier cultivates plots of Chenin, Cabernet Franc and Grolleau Noir with high standards. The terroir is composed of very varied soils: schistose-sandstone soils, veins of quartz and phtannites, volcanic soils: spilites and rhyolites.

2 flagships cuvées : Whaka piripiri and Poïèsis. First one, is truly atypical wine. Exuberant fruit with notes of ripe mango and plum, it is so rich that it is disconcerting. The natural side only comes out on the

finish with a little return to fermentation. Beautiful sensory experience.

Second one, Poïèsis (poetry in Greek) evokes this search for an "ideal" wine (which provokes emotions and which we drink with pleasure). 2 cuvées of Poïèsis in 2018 : 12 months and 24 Months.

Everyone got excited about this estate after a successful first 2017 vintage. 2018 is richer and will certainly need time to express all potential. We are in the presence of a young talent with a promising future. Don't wait ! This gem under radar is rare....

Best 2021 wines

All categories pearls... all is in the title

- Blanc, Champagne Grand Cru, Jérôme Prévost, La Closerie Les Béguines, Extra Brut, 2017 ~ 65 €

Sumptuous champagne of crazy elegance: fine bubble and perfectly supporting a smoky frame with aromas of white-fleshed fruit: white peach, pear but also a finish on fresh almond which sublimates this wine of great precision

- Blanc, Anjou, Thomas Batardière, Esprit Libre 2017 ~ 15 €

Slightly reduced nose, on exotic fruits and honey. Very complex on the palate, aromatic on the roundness, good acidity well controlled, very saline finish. A return to the pear, the passion fruit. Extremely well balanced, it's a bomb....

- Rouge, Beaujolais, Fleurie, Georges Descombes, Vieilles Vignes, 2015 ~ 45 €

Bright red/black color. Beautiful blend of violet, black raspberry, strawberry, and cherry.

Lovely weight here with nice rounded fruit. Crispy juice with formidable precision. very sappy. Top Fleurie, one of the best ever tasted !

Best 2021 Loire wines

The Loire slowly revealed itself as a reference region, especially in the whites. The whites vinified with Chenin are absolutely fantastic. The world is beginning to discover this region which is appreciated and still very much underestimated. You passed near Burgundy in the 2000s before the prices exploded, So, don't miss this train...

- **Blanc, Anjou, Thomas Batardière, Esprit Libre 2017 ~ 15 €**

Slightly reduced nose, on exotic fruits and honey. Very complex on the palate, aromatic on the roundness, good acidity well controlled, very saline finish. A return to the pear, the passion fruit.

Extremely well balanced, it's a bomb....

- **Blanc, Anjou, Clos Des Plantes, Poeisis 2017 ~ 30 €**

On the nose, it is quite complex with notes of honey, pear, mineral but also a beautiful richness which brings greediness. Salty nose, rich on yellow fruits. The mouth keeps all its promises. The palate is round, sapid, apricot, yellow peach, which always remains extremely digestible. Nice finish, good length with a very slight oxidative side very pleasant.

- **Blanc, Savennières, Eric Morgat, Fidès 2016 ~ 45 €**

The lively and lemony nose announces the rest. A clean attack, small notes of butter but it is on the palate that things go right. This chenin expresses its minerality on a bed of citrus fruits (lime, grapefruit) the fullness is magnificent. Some notes of Williams pear enhance the tasting with a great persistence.

Best 2021 Burgundy wines

Ah, Burgundy. Region immensely varied and at the same time so consistent and homogeneous. While Burgundy Bashing begins to appear ... the tastings speak for themselves: this region remains extraordinary in terms of finesse and quality for any wine lover. Some pearls remain sheltered from radars whether on Grands Crus or marginalized appellations. Search, search... Note : some natural wines that emerge here and there despite the economic pressure ...

- **Blanc, Chablis Grand Cru, Domaine de l'Enclos, Les Clos 2018 ~ 60 €**

It is superb, very ripe, round, fat, notes of frangipane, minerality and bitterness marked on the finish

Limpid pale yellow color with pale green reflexes. Very expressive nose of pear and lemon, green apple as primaries, chamomile and wet stone as secondaries to finish in jasmine & honey notes. In mouth, fresh personality, rather a large body in perfect harmony with its acidity, unctuous structure delivering gorgeous citric fruit flavors. Amazing citric & floral aftertaste. Great !

- **Rouge, Santenay 1er cru, Domaine Elodie Roy, Les Gravières 2018 ~ 35 €**

Grapes 100 % de-stemmed, traditional fermentation and maceration offer a beautiful bright ruby red color. Delicate fruity nose cherry, raspberry with a few discrete spice notes

On the palate, the attack is direct with cherry, Medium bodied, the tannins are present and very smooth and balanced. Toasted notes and spices appear on the finish, this 1er Cru boasting complexity and density can challenge much more renowned appellations.

- **Blanc, Corton Charlemagne Grand Cru, Domaine Rollin Père & Fils, 2017 ~ 110 €**

Golden yellow color with very complex nose, honeybee, woody, vanilla, toasted grains, a trail of white fruits. Flint, roasted hazelnuts, lemon. Waouh ! On the palate, perfect, very balanced, a super fine texture. Good length on delicate acidity.

Best 2021 Bordeaux wines

Speculative, too tannic, rarely organic, the wines of Bordeaux are accused of all the evils, to the point that the amateurs turn away from them ... But after this "Bordeaux bashing", would there not be a revival?

- **Rouge, Saint Emilion Grand Cru, Château Mangot 'Todeschini' 2015 ~ 30 €**

40% Cabernet Franc, 30% Cabernet Sauvignon, 30% Merlot. Superb Saint Emilion digestible and elegant, with moderate aging

Mineral nose, black fruits, ripe cassis. Palate: full and complex palate, melted chocolate and mocha concentrated and digestible material, displaying a comfortable stringy chew towards a beautiful final salinity.

- **Rouge, Vin de France, Château Cornélie 2016 ~ 25 €**

Dark garnet color. Meaty nose, exhaling notes of fruit and cocoa combining power and finesse.

On the palate, the wine offers dense and silky tannins, just the right acidity to soften the material. The palate is long and mineral. A racy wine, so elegant.

- **Rouge, Margaux, Château Bel Air Marquis d'Aligre 2010 ~ 45 €**

Patinated garnet color. First extremely precise nose on blackcurrant, truffle, blackcurrant, pepper, tobacco, appear on the finish. It's very pleasant and engaging.

The palate is consistent, very lively, with a slender and elegant style. Very smooth on the palate, but with a significant breadth of persistence on the tertiary aromas of the nose. A special wine by a special winemaker. One of best vintage of the Château.

Best 2021 Rhone wines

One of the oldest vineyards in France and the second largest wine region in France after Bordeaux, Rhone is full of great winegrowers with a lot of various style? At North, great new producers have now solid reputation through Cornas, Crozes Hermitage or of course Côte-Rôtie appellations with wines more or fresher despite climate change. At South, each year we are astonished by variety of style especially in Châteauneuf du Pape with its Old School reputation. Here, forget standards and massive extractions.... Year after year, the Rhône valley widens the circle of its enthusiasts, let's discover !

- **Rouge, Châteauneuf du Pape, Domaine Villeneuve, Vieilles vignes, 2016 ~ 35 €**

Coming from the terroir of Palestor, this chateauneuf is breathtaking.

We find a graceful fruit highlighted by a delicate extraction. The result is a wine in lace, harmonious with its correct acidity awakening the perfect maturity of the berries. Vinification with a minimal dosage of sulfur, we enter the heavens !

- **Rouge, Châteauneuf du Pape, Mas Saint Louis, Les Arpents des Contrebandiers, 2016 ~ 30 €**

Subtle nose of garigues, red fruits, mushrooms and orange zest recall its reputation as a Petit Rayas. Usurped or not, everyone has their own appreciation, but its qualities make it an increasingly sought-after wine. Do not dawdle .... The palate is easy to digest, with a nice freshness without any traces of overripe. The wine is structured but delicate, again like at Domaine de Villeneuve, we are in aerial wines.

- Blanc, Châteauneuf du Pape, Château de la Gardine, Vieilles vignes Cuvée des générations Marie Leoncie, 2017 ~ 45 €

Nose of stone yellow fruits and acacia flowers, with a slight hint of honey and lemon notes on opening.

Exotic fruits then that we find in the mouth combining tension and delicacies. The wine is balanced thanks to a juice that is both chiseled and delicious. No feeling of alcohol. Brilliant!

Best 2021 Alsace wines

It is said that the legibility of Burgundian appellations is complex but what to say about that of Alsace. Another form of complexity. We sometimes get lost in the vintages (How many Grands crus?) Or wines (Is it a dry or a wine with residual sugars?). In short, not easy, on the other hand one thing is clear: the great wines of Alsace are among the best white wines in the world.

- **Rouge, Vin de France, Christophe Lindenlaub, Ami-Amis, 2018 ~ 20 €**

Christophe Lindenlaub is constantly trying to improve himself by experimenting, questioning. This behavior is part of his wines. One of its best cuvées is Ami-Amis. With no sulfur inputs, this wine offers a garnet color with disconcerting farmy aromas followed by sour cherries and baskets of red berries slightly attenuated by Pinot Gris. A unique marriage that delivers a fleshy and dynamic palate thanks to crunchy fruit with just the right acidity.

This is complemented by a superb salinity on the finish. Delicacy ....

- **Blanc, Riesling Alsace Grand Cru Schoenenbourg, Vincent Stoeffler, 2018 ~20 €**

Complex aromas of lemon juice and white fruits, orange blossom, violet and a fine mineral touch. The structure in the mouth is imposing, dry, it is rich and ample. Persistence on the almond paste. A lot of elegance. Finish is long, fresh and saline.

- **Blanc, Alsace Grand Cru 'Altenberg de Bergheim', Marcel Deiss, 2017 ~ 60 €**

Marcel Deiss is one of Alsace's finest producers and this is the top wine in his collection. So not under the radar, but i décided to demonstrate how it is underestimated....

The dress is shiny, golden and oily. The nose is very appealing, with a nice botrytis, pineapple, white flowers, and a nice mineral note. After oxygenation, seductive aromatic blend of musk, citrus oils and herbal essences greets me. On the palate, the wine is mellow but retains a nice freshness which gives it a very nice balance. Vivacity, and primary juiciness make wine vibrant.

Best 2021 Provence & Corse wines

This region with its clement climate for viticulture also changes its last years. Global warming is a challenge. Thus, we see more and more winegrowers reworking old regional grape varieties. The quality has improved enormously in recent years if you take the trouble to look a little, there are gems in the hinterland.

- **Blanc, Coteaux d'Aix en Provence, Henri Milan, La Carrée, 2016 ~ 40 €**

Complex aromas of bitter orange, exotic fruits and mint compose the aromatic bouquet.

Stunning 100% Roussanne wine with great depth of flavor and a lovely rich but soft mouthfeel. No heaviness and sensations of alcohol. South of France demonstrates here that freshness is still possible with climate

- **Rouge, Patrimonio, Domaine Giacometti, Sempre Azezzu, 2014 ~ 20 €**

Grapes are de-stemmed, crushed, and fermented with indigenous yeasts in stainless steel tanks. Purity. No filtration. Generous nose with fresh blueberry, red fruit, barbecue sauce. Tannic and fruity palate, extremely easy to drink. Dangerous top wine, no equivalent in Corsica.

- Rouge, Coteaux d'Aix en Provence, Domaine Abbatucci, Ministre Imperial Cuvée Collection, 2017 ~ 55 €

Farmed biodynamically, flattering nose of red fruit, cocoa, candied cherry which takes us to Corsica. Magic. Supple and soft attack with a slight acidity for a perfect balance.

Deep and complex, with fruits ranging from bright strawberries to dried cranberries. Just density, it lingers on an astonishing earthy and saline finish.

Best 2021 Champagne wines

Champagne is at the dawn of a new era in my opinion. Indeed, the image of the great houses is no longer as strong as it used to be and many great Champagnes from winegrowers are getting noticed. Not that they didn't exist before, but rather that they struggled to make themselves known. Nowadays, digitalization and social networks offer new territory to promote these wines. Finally, these winegrowers are increasingly converting to organic or eco-responsible practices. Without bad puns, this appellation is effervescence....

- Blanc, Champagne Grand Cru, Jérôme Prévost, La Closerie Les Béguines, Extra Brut, 2017 ~ 65 €

Pale golden yellow color. Complex, and attractive nose with toasted bread, aromas of almond slivers, smoky notes, a hint of caramel and a touch of oven-fresh bread. Wine is medium-full bodied with excellent balance between richness, intensity and fresh elegance. structured with its bright, high acidity make this Champagne a very fine, sophisticated Champagne. Merging tradition and modernity in its style, one of the must have Champagne for sure

- Blanc, Champagne, Ruppert-Leroy, Papillon, Brut Nature, 2015 ~ 50 €

Bénédicte Ruppert and Emmanuel Leroy tend 4 hectares of vineyards around Essoyes in the Aube.

Nature Champagne extremely well mastered. Complex notes of almonds, orange, baked apple and red fruits. Nice salty yellow plum nose with some metallic mineral notes, hint of florals. A clean but smooth attack builds on a powerful body. Great acidity structure to pass a decade with a lot of refreshing salinity and tonicity.

- Blanc, Champagne Grand Cru, Hebrart, Rive Gauche Rive Droite, Extra Brut, 2013 ~ 50 €

Blend of Pinot Noir from Aÿ and Chardonnay from Oiry, Chouilly and Avize, all Grand Crus. Note of white peach, apple, a fine base of soil, fresh-baked bread. Scents of stewed fruit and milk caramel. Lively attack giving way to a structured and ample body. Tasty, energetic palate with great depth. Outstanding gourmet champagne.

Best 2021 Jura & Savoie wines

What global enthusiasm for this region so close to and at the same time so distinct from its sister Burgundy. Savoie, a little behind, also testifies to a more recent highlight.

Here, the wines are borrowed from purity and minerality and biodynamic vinification works wonders, try these few bottles ...

- **Blanc, Domaine Gilles Berlioz, Chignin-Bergeron 'Cuvée Les Christine', 2019 ~ 65 €**

What a Roussanne from Savoie !

The nose is complex and expressive with notes of exotic fruits (lychee and fresh pineapple), white fruits but also humus and white flowers. By dwelling on this one we move on to roasted notes evoking grilled almonds and puffed rice.

The mouth, ultra-balanced and salivating, blooms on a wide body, an explosive volume. The matter is concentrated and channeled by a tight acidity. No heaviness, balance between fat and mineral tension. To cellar for eternity ....

- Blanc, Domaine des Marnes Blanches, Savagnin Aux Bois, 2017 ~ 18 €

Color is light gold. Very intense, the nose presents expected aromas of fresh nuts, pear, exotic fruits, marzipan and yellow fruits. The attack presents a light fatness but very quickly it develops a superb freshness imbued with minerality. The palate is endowed with a beautiful volume, gaining in width and length with oxygenation. The wine is powerful but counterbalanced by an acidity which lengthens the wine. Excellent

- Blanc, Domaine Kevin Bouillet, Pépin Blanc, 2018 les zinszins du vins ~ 19 €

Kevin Bouillet took over a few hectares of family vines around Pupillin in 2018. He vinifies as naturally as possible. Massal selections of Red Tailed Melon.

Nose on citrus and white fruits. The palate is fleshy with ample substance. The dynamism of this wine combined with the breadth of the juice of the Red-tailed Melon grape variety gives it surprising drinkability.

Best 2021 Languedoc Roussillon wines

The wines of Languedoc Roussillon have always been a source of great wines. There are great winemakers with moderate notoriety on French territory but who are struggling to make themselves known beyond the borders. And yet .... This region does not arouse the same enthusiasm as others sometimes because of the lack of finesse or a too alcoholic imprint. Here all the other way around, here are three of the most beautiful bottles from the region for this year which shows that there are great winemakers.

- **Rouge, Vin de France, Maximus de la Pascole, 2018 ~ 35 €**

Joint work of two amazing winemakers Nicolas Carmarans and Bruno Duchene to offer this whole harvest wine with minimal intervention. Aging in Burgundy rooms. Not glued or filtered, zero sulfur.

Notes of raspberry, fig, juniper and spices, juice of beautiful color, medium bodied with a savory fruit with velvety tannins.

- Rouge, Les Terrasses d'Elises, Rouge, le Pradel, 2018 ~ 25 €

A real basket of red fruits complemented by notes of lychee, flowers and citrus fruits. Greedy mouth from the start thanks to a subtle sweetness, a delicate lace texture marked by tangy fruit. It's tasty without tiring thanks to its freshness, typical of Cinsault grape. This wine never leaves anyone indifferent with its remarkable finesse ...

- Rouge, Corbières, Maxime Magnon, Rouge, 2018 5 20 €

Nose on the animal, blueberry, cherry. The attack is fluid and supple.

The palate is powerful but also delicate in its structure thanks to fine and powdery tannins. The wine is very easy to digest, far from the clichés of alcoholic and heavy Corbières wines.

Best 2021 Beaujolais wines

In the 1980s, when pesticides and other chemicals were the norm in the vines and tanks, young winegrowers tried their hand at remaking the wine of their ancestors. A shift in quality then began again and today the Beaujolais has become a determining region in the wine landscape. These winegrowers like Lapierre and Métras have restored the image of the region and inspired other generations. Also, the tastes for the wines on finesse and digestibility only accentuated the attraction for this region. We thus find high quality wines on styles now very varied as you most certainly know. Here are some gems that are either unknown or not recognized enough.

- **Rouge, Beaujolais, Julienas, Les Bertrand, Pur Ju…, 2019 ~ 20 €**

Brambly red fruits, currants, red cherries, plums and fine spices.

Juicy, very fine and fresh, fine caressing tannins. Mineral structure which is accentuated on the finish.

Lots of depth and personality in this emotional wine. From my opinion, one of best and consistent wine from Yann Bertrand.

- Rouge, Beaujolais, Brouilly, Pierre Cotton, 2018 ~ 22 €

Nose a little bit yeast character, juicy cranberry, sour strawberry and raspberry.

Fresh with nice brightness, direct, lovely purity. Wine is vivid with a grippy, spicy edge.

Great bottle by a promising winemaker.

- Rouge, Beaujolais, Fleurie, Georges Descombes, Vieilles Vignes, 2015 ~ 45 €

Bright red/black color. Beautiful blend of violet, black raspberry, strawberry, and cherry.

Lovely weight here with a nice rounded fruit. Crispy juice with formidable precision. Very sappy. Top Fleurie, one of the best ever tasted!

Best 2021 Sud Ouest wines

The South-West has some 50,000 hectares of vines. The wide range of wines and grape varieties of this vineyard make it endearing and full of surprises. New winegrowers have come to shake up the codes and make great wines at very affordable prices compared to the leading regions of France.

- **Blanc, Irouléguy, Domaine Pantxuri Arretxea – Schistes 2017 ~ 40 €**

Expressive notes of ripe fruit with oxidative yeast & mineral saline. Powerfully full-bodied white underlined by high acidity and salted-mineral bitterness finish Intricate.

Ultra-tracing and salivating, this wine shakes up by letting the terroir speak here.

- **Rouge, Cahors, Mas Del Perié de Fabien Jouves – Bloc B763 2017 ~ 50 €**

Plot cuvée aged 16 months in concrete egg.

Notes of cherry, blackcurrant, leather, pepper, the fruit then fades to give way to some mineral touches.

Clean attack delivering a harmonious and dense substance. The acidity underlines this beautiful juice with silky and powdery tannins.

Good length.

- **Blanc, Jurançon, Domaine Camin Larredya – Costa Blanca 2017 ~ 50 €**

Notes of white fruits, honey, beeswax, ginger, papaya and white pepper. Full, voluminous, straight and rich, dry in the mouth, it delivers touches of candied pineapple on a fresh and balanced background. Tight, chiseled, vibrant, my biggest dry Jurançon. Fantastic winemaker.

Best 2021 Rosé wine

- Rosé, Coteaux d'Aix en Provence, Domaine de Sulauze, Pomponette, 2019 ~ 12 €

Pale pink in color with aromatics that are bright and clear. The Rolle grappe is here sublime. It is wonderfully crisp and flavorful on the palate with medium body and notes of red berries on the finish.

No bitterness or exuberance. Total balance. Certainly, one of the best rosé of the year.

Best 2021 Quality Price wine

- Blanc, Anjou, Thomas Batardière, Esprit Libre 2017
  ~ 15 €

Slightly reduced nose, on exotic fruits and honey. Very complex on the palate, aromatic on the roundness, good acidity well controlled, very saline finish. A return to the pear, the passion fruit.

Extremely well balanced, it is a bomb....

Printed in Great Britain
by Amazon

62583135R00020